A CAMBRIDGE TOPIC BOOK

Muslim Spain

Duncan Townson

Published in cooperation with Cambridge University Press
Lerner Publications Company, Minneapolis

Editors' Note: In preparing this edition of *The Cambridge Topic Books* for publication, the editors have made only a few minor changes in the original material. In some isolated cases, British spelling and usage were altered in order to avoid possible confusion for our readers. Whenever necessary, information was added to clarify references to people, places, and events in British history. An index was also provided in each volume.
In this book, accents in Spanish and Arabic words have been omitted for the sake of simplicity.

LIBRARY OF CONGRESS CATALOGING IN PUBLICATION DATA

Townson, Duncan.
Muslim Spain.

(A Cambridge Topic Book)
Includes index.
SUMMARY: Details that period of Spanish history and civilization when the Muslims invaded and took over the Iberian peninsula, parts of which they controlled for nearly 800 years.

1. Spain—Civilization—711-1492—Juvenile literature. 2. Arabs in Spain—Juvenile literature. [1. Spain—Civilization—711-1492. 2. Arabs in Spain] I. Title.

DP103.5.T68 1979   946'.02   78-56805
ISBN 0-8225-1216-5

This edition first published 1979 by Lerner Publications Company
by permission of Cambridge University Press.

Original edition copyright © 1973 by Cambridge University Press
as part of *The Cambridge Introduction to the History of Mankind: Topic Book.*

International Standard Book Number: 0-8225-1216-5
Library of Congress Catalog Card Number: 78-56805

Manufactured in the United States of America.

This edition is available exclusively from:
Lerner Publications Company, 241 First Avenue North, Minneapolis, Minnesota 55401

Contents

Dates

AD

570	The birth of the Prophet Muhammad
622	The Hijra. The flight of Muhammad to Medina.
632	The death of Muhammad
635–41	Muslims conquer Syria, Palestine, Persia & Egypt
661	Umayyads become rulers of the Islamic Empire
711	Muslims invade Spain
732	Battle of Tours
750	Abbasids become rulers of the Islamic Empire
756–88	Abd al-Rahman I rules Spain
762	Baghdad founded
822–52	Abd al-Rahman II
912–61	Abd al-Rahman III
961–76	Al-Hakam II
1002	Death of al-Mansur
1031	End of the caliphate of Cordoba
1085	Christians capture Toledo
1212	Battle of Las Navas de Tolosa
1236	Ferdinand III of Castile captures Cordoba
1492	Ferdinand & Isabella conquer Granada

1. The Arabs conquer Spain

The Prophet Muhammad

Muhammad (his name means 'worthy of praise') was born in Mecca about AD 570. His father died before his birth and his mother when he was six, so he was brought up as an orphan, first by his grandfather and then by his uncle. He probably accompanied his uncle on trading journeys to Syria and later became the agent of a wealthy business-woman, Khadija, who was a widow. She was impressed by his ability and honesty and eventually they were married.

In Mecca the great merchants put business and their own wealth before everything else. The weaker members of the community, such as widows and orphans, were neglected. Though he was now a rich merchant himself, Muhammad felt deeply that this greed and heartlessness were very wrong. Worrying about the troubles of Mecca made Muhammad often want to be alone to think, so he used to go to a cave in one of the barren, rocky hills near Mecca, often thinking and praying for several days and nights at a time. During these lonely nights he began to have strange experiences, vivid dreams. Once a mighty Being appeared in the sky. He thought this was God, and then he thought it was the Angel Gabriel. Muhammad was so terrified that he almost committed suicide, but he got over this and became convinced, perhaps by the encouragement of his wife, that he had received a genuine message from heaven. He felt that he had been given a special task by God and that he was, indeed, 'God's messenger'.

From this time onwards, until the end of his life Muhammad had more such revelations from God. The earliest messages appear to have been short sentences in praise of God. They also warned of the terrors of the Last Judgement, when the Lord would reward and punish each according to his deeds. To escape Hell, the eternal fire, the sinner must be sorry for his evil deeds and throw himself on the mercy of God. The name of the new religion was, and is, Islam. The word means submission, complete obedience to the will of God.

Muhammad told his message to some relatives and close friends and they were the first to accept him as a prophet of God. But when Muhammad began to preach in the streets of Mecca, he met with scorn and anger. By 622 Mecca was so dangerous that he had to flee to Medina, a town 250 miles to the north where the people believed his teachings and fought for him. In 630 Muhammad returned to Mecca in triumph. More and more people accepted the religion of Islam and became Muslims, as believers in Islam are called.

In 632 Muhammad died. He left no son, so his old and trusted friend, Abu Bakr, was chosen to lead the Muslims. The people greeted him as 'khalifa' (caliph), the 'successor' of the Prophet. He did not have any religious authority, because Muslims believed that Muhammad had been the final prophet and had completed God's message to mankind. The caliph was the Commander of the Faithful, the protector of Muslims and their leader in war.

We do not have any pictures of the Arabs who invaded Spain but they may have looked like this Arab horseman, drawn in the tenth century.

The Arab Empire

When Muhammad died only Arabia was Muslim but in 633 Bedouin warriors from the deserts of Arabia began to move beyond their northern borders. Within ten years they created a huge Arab Empire which included Syria, Iraq, Persia and Egypt. It was probably a surprise to the Arabs themselves that what had begun as raids for plunder became permanent conquests. The speed and vastness of these conquests were amazing. Nomads with no military experience beyond desert skirmishes and bandit raids had defeated the regular armies of two great empires, Byzantium and Persia.

After these early conquests there was a lull. The Arabs had to organise their new lands, and quarrels broke out as to who was to be caliph. This led to a civil war between 656 and 661, when the Umayyads (the family of Umar, or Omar) gained control. They were a branch of the tribe to which the Prophet Muhammad had belonged, and were to rule for nearly a hundred years. The capital of the empire was now moved to Damascus in Syria and was never again to be in Arabia, though Medina and, especially, Mecca remained for Muslims the most holy of cities.

The second age of conquest took place under the Umayyads, who doubled the size of the empire by carrying the holy war into North Africa, Western Europe and the heart of Asia. This advance was even more surprising than the first, as the new conquests were so much further from Arabia, and in places where the people were very different from the Arabs.

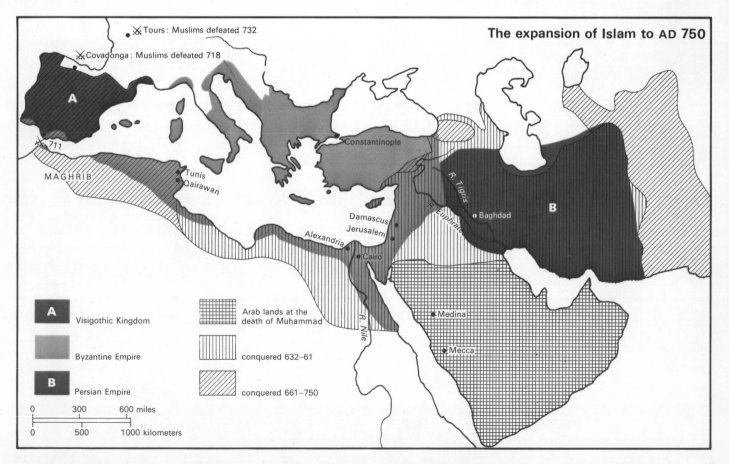

The expansion of Islam to AD 750

Tours: Muslims defeated 732
Covadonga: Muslims defeated 718
711
MAGHRIB
Tunis
Qairawan
Constantinople
Damascus
Jerusalem
Alexandria
Cairo
R. Tigris
R. Euphrates
Baghdad
B
Medina
Mecca
R. Nile
A

| A | Visigothic Kingdom |
| Byzantine Empire |
| B | Persian Empire |

Arab lands at the death of Muhammad
conquered 632–61
conquered 661–750

0   300   600 miles
0   500   1000 kilometers

above: The way of life of the Bedouin has changed little. This nomad tent in the Tunisian desert is like those the Arabs lived in when they were conquering North Africa and Spain.

above right: A mosaic in the Umayyad palace of Khirbat al-Mafjar, Jordan, built in AD 743-4. Roman influence can be seen in the abstract border patterns while the tree and animals are more eastern in style.

right: Ruins of the Umayyad city of Anjar (ninth century AD) in the Lebanon. Again you can see Roman influence in the shape of the pillars and arches as well as in the regular layout of streets.

The first of the territories to be conquered in this new wave of invasions was North Africa, the lands between Egypt and the Atlantic, which the Arabs called the Maghrib (Arabic for west). This area had been part of the Byzantine Empire. Now the Byzantine fleet could not use the North African ports and its nearest bases were in Sicily. Therefore, when the Muslims had conquered the land which lay opposite Spain, across the narrow straits, there were no hostile warships to stop them from going further.

Spain under the Visigoths

The wealth of Spain, especially the silver, tin and copper, had for centuries attracted foreign merchants and settlers — for example Greeks and Carthaginians. Spain was peaceful and prosperous as part of the Roman Empire, but with the barbarian invasions of the fifth century, the country was occupied by tribes of Germanic warriors who tried to make themselves lords over the ordinary people still working in town and country. One such tribe were the Vandals, after whom the Arabs were to name Spain 'al-Andalus'. But the Vandals were soon pushed out by other tribes, one of which, the Visigoths, took control of Spain in 456.

Now, two and a half centuries later, the Visigothic state was rotten. The feeble king could not protect the peasants (who were not of Visigothic blood) against the great landlords, whose vast estates covered two-thirds of the land. The Visigoth lords paid no taxes and lived in luxury, while the peasants went hungry. Many peasants and slaves had run away from their masters, formed robber bands and terrorised the countryside. In the towns the Jews, many of them important merchants and craftsmen, were equally angry and anxious. A decree of 681 said that all Jews had to become Christian (because this was now the religion of the Visigothic rulers) or leave the country. A further order of 694 said that those who remained should be sold into slavery, except for their children under seven, who were to be brought up as Christians. Even the Visigothic nobles weakened the state, constantly squabbling amongst themselves. King Witiza died in 710. There followed a struggle for the throne between his son and Roderic, one of the nobles.

Visigothic coinage: a gold solidus showing the head of King Wamba who ruled AD 672–80. Diameter $\frac{3}{4}$ in (18mm).

The Arabs attack

The Visigoths, then, were fighting a civil war when the Muslims made a small raid on the coast of al-Andalus in 710. The opposition was so weak and the booty so attractive that Musa, the governor of North Africa, organised a larger expedition. It was composed mainly of Berbers from North Africa, under the command of his Berber freedman Tarik. In 711 he landed with 7000 men at the foot of the mighty rock which bears his name, Gibraltar (from Jabal Tarik, the mountain of Tarik). Moving west he took up a strong position on the River Barbate and there waited for the Visigothic army, led by Roderic. It arrived tired after a long march from the North. On one day the fate of Spain was decided for centuries. The bishop of Seville, brother of Witiza, fought on the Muslim side. Part of the Visigothic army deserted, the rest was crushed and Roderic disappeared forever, probably drowned and swept out to sea.

Tarik then marched rapidly on the towns of southern Spain. The peasants had no desire to fight for their lords. The Jews welcomed the invaders, who left them to garrison towns as the Muslim army moved forward. The victories were so easy and the booty so great that Tarik ignored Musa's orders not to plunge far inside Spain. He pushed on to the capital, Toledo, which he captured. Starting in the spring, he had by the end of the summer become master of half of Spain – there had been no swifter conquest even in the astonishing record of Islam. Musa, jealous of the victories of his Berber commander, came himself in 712 with an Arab army. Near Toledo, he caught up with Tarik. As Tarik stepped forward to receive his commander with due honours, Musa slashed him across the face with his whip and put him in chains for disobeying orders. Under Musa the conquest went on as easily as before and by 714 all organised resistance was over.

The remaining Visigothic soldiers had been driven into the wild mountain glens of Asturias in the north, a poor and thinly populated land. Here they held out under a leader called Pelayo. In 718, at Covadonga, he defeated a small Muslim force. Arab writers made light of the affair. 'A wild ass', they said, 'reared up against the Muslims. They defeated his army time and time again until nothing remained of it but thirty men and two women and these lived on the wild honey that they found in clefts of the rocks. At last the Muslims wearied of them and would not be bothered longer, saying "What harm can thirty wild asses do us?"' Nevertheless, the Arabs never held this northern part of Spain.

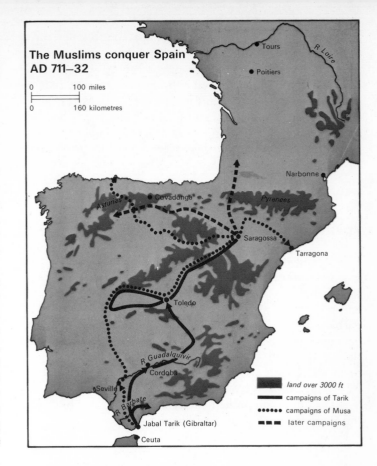

The Muslims conquer Spain
AD 711–32

0 — 100 miles
0 — 160 kilometres

land over 3000 ft
————— campaigns of Tarik
•••••••• campaigns of Musa
– – – – later campaigns

A triumphant return

Meanwhile, in distant Damascus the Caliph al-Walid recalled Musa to explain why he had acted without his permission. Musa, therefore, slowly made his way overland to Syria, accompanied by his officers, and by 400 Visigothic princes, wearing crowns and gold belts. These were followed by vast numbers of slaves and prisoners of war, loaded with treasure. His triumphant march through North Africa was like the victorious processions of the great Roman generals. In 715 Musa entered Damascus and was greeted by al-Walid. The official reception, held with great dignity and pomp in the courtyard of the Great Mosque, must have been one of the most splendid ceremonies in the history of Islam. For the first time, Muslims saw hundreds of European princes and thousands of ordinary folk doing homage to the Commander of the Faithful, the head of Islam. Musa, however, suffered for being too successful. Al-Walid was sick when Musa arrived in Damascus and soon died. His successor was jealous of Musa and humiliated him by making him stand in the sun till he was exhausted. He then confiscated Musa's property and took away from him all his authority. The last we hear of the conqueror of the Maghrib and al-Andalus (North Africa and Spain) is as a beggar in a remote village of Arabia.

Spain was now a province of the caliphate, ruled by a governor appointed by the caliph in Damascus.

The courtyard of the Great Mosque in Damascus, Syria, with its square minaret. Begun in 706, it is one of the earliest Muslim buildings to survive, though little of the original mosque remains. It is here that Musa was received by the Caliph.

The battle of Tours

Spain quickly became a base for yet further attacks on Christian Europe. In France there were many rich churches and monasteries, which were tempting prey to Arabs and Berbers in search of loot. A series of expeditions began which carried the Arabs across the mountains of the Pyrenees into southern France, where cities were raided, plundered and burned. The last and greatest of these expeditions was in 732, when a large Arab army crossed the Pyrenees and marched along the old Roman road to the Loire, aiming at the wealthy shrine of St Martin at Tours. Between that town and Poitiers they met the Frankish army of Charles Martel ('the Hammer'). For seven days the armies watched each other. There were skirmishes. At last the Arabs attacked. The Frankish warriors formed a hollow square and stood shoulder to shoulder, firm as a wall. They hewed down with their swords the Arab cavalry — among their victims was the Muslim commander — until darkness at last separated the two armies. At dawn the next day there was no sound from the place where the Arabs had camped. Charles suspected a trick. He sent spies to find out. Under cover of night the Arabs had quietly packed their tents and vanished. Charles was left victorious.

There has been much argument about the importance of this battle of Tours or Poitiers. Arab historians call it 'the way of martyrs' because the Muslims' losses were so heavy, but the Frankish losses too were heavy and Charles Martel was not able to follow up his victory. Edward Gibbon, writing in eighteenth-century England, imagined what would have happened if the Arabs had won that battle. They would, he thought, have reached the Rhine and the English Channel and would have sailed up the Thames. There would be mosques in London and Paris where cathedrals now stand, and 'the Koran would now be taught in the schools of Oxford'. Other historians say that the battle decided little. The Arab invasion, already a thousand miles advanced from Gibraltar, had lost its force and come to a halt, except for raids for booty.

Whatever the truth of this argument, Poitiers does mark the furthest limit of Muslim advance in the West. Soon the Muslim forces would be pushed out of France (they lost their main base in southern France, Narbonne, in 759) and confined to Spain. There they were to stay for 700 years and were to build a civilisation unequalled in Western Christendom.

9

2. Abd al-Rahman I

The Abbasids

In 750 a new family came to rule the Islamic Empire. The Abbasids (so-called because they were descended from the Prophet Muhammad's uncle Abbas) seized power and set up in Baghdad their own dynasty, which was to last for 500 years. The new caliph was represented in Syria by an uncle, who called himself al-Saffah – the shedder of blood – the generous host who takes pride in slaughtering cattle to entertain his guests. He now justified his name in a new and grimmer sense. Every member of the Umayyad family he could find he killed or mutilated.

The remaining Umayyads went into hiding, until al-Saffah promised to spare their lives. About eighty survivors believed his promise and accepted an invitation to a banquet. 'As they arrived, al-Saffah gathered them in his tent, and when all were there, he took Abd al-Wahid' – the senior member present – 'and made him sit next to him as if to show the gratitude which the Abbasids owed them, and talked to him of that matter and made great cheer. Then he made a sign to the guards who stood behind them and said, "Beat their heads in", and at once they were killed with clubs. Then he said to Abd al-Wahid, "There is no reason why you should outlive your kinsfolk and their power, but I will allow you to die by the sword", and they beheaded him. And others say that he had leather covers (the usual covering for a dinner table) spread over the bodies of the dead men and feasted on them.'

Abd al-Rahman escapes

Abd al-Rahman, grandson of an Ummayad Caliph, was wise enough not to attend this banquet but stayed on his farm near the River Euphrates. Suddenly his younger brother saw the black standards of the Abbasids appear and warned Abd al-Rahman. They snatched up some money, galloped to the Euphrates and plunged in. The Abbasid soldiers followed them and called them back, saying they had nothing to fear. Abd al-Rahman gave his own account of what happened next.

'I continued to swim with my brother a little behind me. I turned to help him and encourage him, but alas! on hearing those words of peace he turned back for fear of drowning, hastening to his death. I called to him, "Come here beloved" but God did not will that he should hear me and he went back. Some of the enemy began to strip and swim after me but they gave up and took the boy and cut his head off before me. He was thirteen years old. May God have pity on him! I went on.'

For five years Abd al-Rahman wandered in disguise through Palestine, Egypt and North Africa. All the time, moving from tribe to tribe and town to town, friendless and penniless, he had to be on his guard against Abbasid spies and narrowly escaped arrest and execution in the Maghrib. Finally in 755 he reached Ceuta, on the North African coast opposite Spain, where he was offered protection by some Berbers who were related to his mother.

Master of Cordoba

From there he made contact with Arabs in al-Andalus, many of whom came from Syria, like Abd al-Rahman himself, and were Umayyad supporters. With their help he invaded Spain, to find that city after city opened its gates to him without resistance. He soon became master of Spain, much to the annoyance of the Abbasid Caliph in Baghdad. In 761 the caliph appointed a new governor of Spain. This made Abd al-Rahman furious. He captured the governor, cut off his head and sent it, preserved in salt and camphor and wrapped in a black flag, with his certificate of appointment, to the caliph, who was on a pilgrimage to Mecca. 'Thank God for putting the sea between us and this devil of a foe', said the caliph, on receiving his grisly present.

Abd al-Rahman's troubles were by no means over. The country was rarely at peace, as the northern frontier was always on fire or smouldering. The frontier was not a fixed line but a wide area of desolation, into which Christian or Muslim lords led their armies, whenever peace at home left their hands free. Later, as the Christian leaders gathered strength, they built castles at strategic points and gradually extended their hold round these bases. This was the birth of Castile, the land of the castles. But at this time, and for many years to come, the Christians in the north were not so much a serious danger as an expense and annoyance.

Peñafiel Castle near the River Douro, is one of the castles which gives Castile its name. It was the site of a Christian castle from the tenth century. Captured by the Muslims in 995, it was reconquered by Sancho Garcia for the Christians. He planted his lance on top of the hill saying, 'From now on this will be the Faithful Rock (Peñafiel) of Castile'. The present castle dates from the fifteenth century.

Even in his capital of Cordoba, however, Abd al-Rahman could not relax. After obtaining the throne he had to spend much of his time defending it against the plots of the Berbers, who claimed that the best land was given to the Arabs and not to them, and the plots of some dissatisfied Arabs who were Abbasid supporters. He had to put down plots and revolts right up to the time of his death.

Abd al-Rahman became a tyrant. The ruler who had once been so popular dared not stroll through the streets of Cordoba. To make sure of his safety he sent to Africa for Berbers to form his bodyguard. He paid them well and they were loyal, so he kept his throne. He ruled in defiance of the caliph in Baghdad – al-Andalus was the first part of the Muslim world to become independent of the caliphate – but contented himself with the title of amir or commander.

His life was summed up in a story of Abd al-Rahman's enemy, the Abbasid Caliph Mansur. One day he asked his friends, 'Who is the Falcon of the Quraysh?' (The Quraysh was the Prophet Muhammad's tribe from which all the caliphs claimed descent.) They claimed that it was Mansur himself, the Commander of the Faithful, because he organised the Islamic

Empire, put down revolts and gave peace to men's minds. Then they suggested other caliphs but he said, 'It is Abd al-Rahman, who first by cunning escaped from the spears and swords of his enemies, crossed the desert and the sea, entered a land of Unbelievers, founded cities, gathered armies and with his good government and firmness of character built an empire in a lawless country ... The Commander of the Faithful had the support of his family and followers: but Abd al-Rahman was alone, with nothing to aid him but his wits and no supporter but his unshakable will.'

The ruling house established by Abd al-Rahman I, lasted for nearly 300 years. Throughout this period Cordoba was the capital and, particularly in the tenth century, the city enjoyed a period of incomparable splendour as the western rival of Baghdad. It was the most powerful state in Europe, courted by neighbours and distant rulers alike. This increase in power was shown when Abd al-Rahman III finally took the title caliph in 929. Till then this name had only been used by the rulers of the Islamic Empire in the East, centred on Baghdad.

11

3. Cordoba: Jewel of the World

The city of Cordoba had been a thriving place long before the time of the Romans. Under their rule it developed into a prosperous city, and produced many notable people including the philosopher Seneca and the poet Lucan. Cordoba was well situated to be a capital city. The River Guadalquivir (its name comes from the Arabic Wadi al-kabir, 'long valley'), the longest in Spain, passes there through a broad fertile plain which could produce food for a growing population. From there it runs through good agricultural land and passes Seville before it reaches the sea. The approaches to Cordoba are easily defended: to both south and north the city is protected by mountain ranges.

By the tenth century, when Cordoba was at the height of its fame, it had a population of half a million. It also had, according to Arab historians, 113,000 houses, 700 mosques, 300 public baths, 70 libraries and numerous bookshops. And all this, when there was no city in Western Christendom with a population of 10,000.

The traveller who entered the city from the south would cross the river by the old Roman bridge and pass under the arch of the southern gate. There were great fortified gates on each side of the city with roads connecting each gate though, as you can see from the map, these were not like the straight roads which the Romans used to make. In fact, as smaller

The Roman bridge at Cordoba. On the islets in the river there were water wheels which kept the city supplied with water. In the foreground is part of a later water wheel.

opposite:
The map shows the network of streets within the walls. 'Suburbs' extended along the river to east and west.

lanes grew out of these roads without any system, the resulting 'plan' was a maze of narrow alleys.

But the traveller from the south would not immediately be plunged into this maze for he would come first of all to the walls of the palace of the amirs on his left and on his right the walls of the Great Mosque, the 'church' of the Muslims. Of the palace which the amirs built (on the site of the palace of earlier Visigothic governors) little can now be seen because the king's castle and the palace of the Christian bishops were later built on the same site. But it was a splendid building with many courts and fountains, gardens, baths, stables and out-houses. You can see from the drawing on the next page how elaborately the rooms were decorated and other pictures in this chapter give some idea of the kind of things that would be in them.

A view of the fertile valley of the Guadalquivir and its surrounding hills. The photograph is taken from the towers of the alcazar which the Christian kings began in 1328 to replace that of the Muslim amirs and caliphs. (Al-kasr is Arabic for castle.)

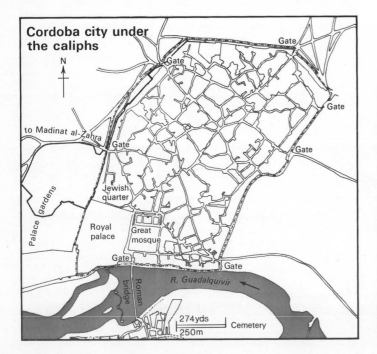

The Court of Oranges of the Great Mosque at Cordoba. People washed in the wells here before they went into the mosque to pray. The great belfry you can see on the right was a Christian addition made in the seventeenth century, long after the mosque had become a cathedral.

Story tellers in Muslim countries still attract large and attentive audiences, as they did in Muslim Spain. Here is one in Marrakesh, Morocco.

The Great Mosque does still stand and there is later in this book a whole chapter describing it (pages 36-9). Although it was first of all a building for worship, the mosque also provided a place where people could meet and talk. Here the traveller would go on his arrival, to find his way and pick up the news. In the evening the mosque courtyards with their trees and fountains were a welcome relief for the citizens of Cordoba too. Here was a breath of fresh air after the narrow streets with their stinking drains between the high blank house walls.

At the city gates and at the crossing of the main roads there were other open spaces where people could meet, hold a market, or a celebration, or listen to a story just as they do in Moorish cities today.

left: A modern artist's idea of a festival in the palace of the amirs at Cordoba.

Houses and gardens

The houses of the poorer people had walls of unbaked brick, dried in the sun. The roof was made of interlaced branches plastered with clay and made waterproof, to some extent, by a mixture of lime and ashes. This was not very effective but good enough for a land where rain was rare.

Here and there was a larger house of two stories, belonging to a merchant perhaps, and sometimes a mansion standing in its own grounds. These richer houses had large gardens but, like the poorer dwellings, had little to attract the attention of the passer-by from the outside. The house plan was the same as in present-day Muslim cities. A small door opened onto a passage, which led to an open courtyard with rooms around it. This courtyard would be rectangular and might be overlooked by a gallery from an upper floor. Here the master of the house attended to business and received visitors. In the houses of the wealthy there would be a further courtyard for the women. Both courts would normally have a fountain in the middle and orange and lemon trees in beds that ran parallel to the sides. Such houses had efficient drainage

Ground floor plan of a typical house in Muslim Cordoba; (a)–(d) are rooms opening on to an inner courtyard; (x) marks the position of the lattice-work grilles which took the place of windows.

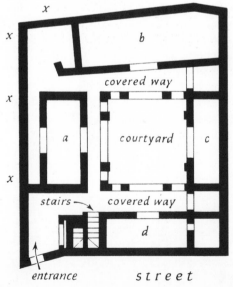

Above is one of the three tenth-century minarets which still stand in Cordoba. It is now the tower of a Christian church.

systems, though the drains would not go further than the street outside. Even poorer houses often had lavatories with water drainage, something which was not found at that time in other cities of western Europe. The furniture in rooms was rather sparse as people mostly sat on cushions on the carpeted floor and food was served on little low tables.

Muslim Cordoba had many features which were to be found nowhere else in Europe outside Byzantium. It had miles of paved streets, illuminated by lights from bordering houses. Seven hundred years later there was not so much as one public lamp in London and paving was almost unknown. When the

A typical inner courtyard of a house in Cordoba is shown on the left, with its vines, plants and arched portico for shade. This is similar to the courtyards of Muslim houses in the tenth century. Beyond the walls of the houses were narrow streets, like the one above, though nowadays there are more windows and balconies.

Western Christians still looked on having a bath as a heathen custom, the people of Cordoba had been enjoying public baths for generations. Public baths were very popular among the Muslims and were similar to the baths of the Romans. Because of this the Arabs called them 'hammam al-Rumi' which means 'Roman baths'. The baths were built on a plan that is still found in the Middle East. There was a room for undressing, then a series of rooms, each hotter than the last, and finally a cooler room where, covered in towels, the bather spent an hour cooling off so that he could go outside. In the afternoon the baths were used by women and a cloth was placed over the entrance, to remind the men to keep out. For hours the women relaxed and gossiped there and took along with them their slaves and make-up specialists.

Another recreation for rich and poor alike was getting together for picnics and garden parties. People in Cordoba had a passion for them and any occasion would do. Marriages and circumcisions – all Muslim boys were circumcised – called for splendid celebrations. Then there were the Muslim and Christian feast days. At the Christian feast of the Epiphany the whole population joined in torch-lit processions that went on all night. There were saint's day pilgrimages to Christian monasteries where the monks gave lavish hospitality. Muslims who might have felt worried about drinking more wine than their religion allowed, excused themselves by arguing that out of respect for their hosts they could not refuse.

The feast days were the great occasions. For other days there was the garden party in the country. Every rich family owned a country house: the whole plain between Cordoba and the mountain range of the Sierra Morena, to the north of the city, was carpeted with them. Abd al-Rahman I set the fashion with his farm at Rusafa.

Later Abd al-Rahman III moved his whole court out of the city to al-Zahra about 5 miles away. The palace he built there was partly a fortress and partly a country house of 400 rooms. There were three descending terraces, each high above the rest to give a clear view of the surrounding country. Turreted walls protected each terrace. On the upper terrace was the caliph's palace; the middle terrace consisted of shaded gardens, orchards and a game reserve; the lower terrace contained the living quarters of slaves and servants (17,000 of them), barracks for the guards, workshops, a mint, public baths and a large mosque, which overlooked the River

Almost nothing remains of the once magnificent palace of Madinat al-Zahra. It was destroyed by Berbers who revolted in 1013. Above you can see part of the reconstruction of the great hall of the caliph. The bits of broken masonry lying on the floor show how much has still to be done.

Guadalquivir. To give an abundant supply of water, Abd al-Rahman tunnelled through the nearby hills and built an aqueduct.

One of the wonders of al-Zahra was the Room of the Caliphs, which had a gilded ceiling and walls of many-coloured marble blocks. On each side of the hall were eight doors decorated with gold and ebony and inlaid with precious stones. These doors stood between columns of coloured marble and clear crystal. In the centre of the room was a large pool filled with mercury. When the sun shone into the room and was reflected from the walls and roof, it produced a dazzling effect. Here the caliph received foreign ambassadors. If he wanted to amaze his visitors, he would signal to one of his slaves to disturb the pool, 'and at once the whole room was shot through with rays of light, which reduced those present to terror, as the whole hall seemed to be floating away, so long as the mercury went on quivering'. Although their accounts differ in several details, all the writers at the time agreed that the magnificence of this hall had never been equalled.

Of course the gardens and the picnics of the ordinary people were simpler affairs but everyone wanted to spend the long summer days in the carefully laid out gardens that the Arabs liked so much: with the channels of running water and paths sanded, or paved with bricks on edge to form patterns. Their ideal was described by the poet Ibn Hazm: flower beds overlooking a wide view, little streams crossing one another like swords of silver, birds singing full-throated, fruit ready to be plucked, shady branches screening the sun's rays, flowers of many colours stirred by the fragrant breeze. He imagined the spring sun not too strong, veiled by a mist of light rain, like a shy girl hiding herself from jealous eyes. This was the earthly paradise the Arabs, once dwellers in the sun-scorched desert, loved to imagine and to make real when they lived in lush land like that around Cordoba. To this day the Muslim influence on Spanish gardens continues, as you can see from this picture of the gardens of the Generalife in Granada.

At these garden parties the guests did not eat one course after another. The whole dinner was put on display at once and guests helped themselves to whatever they liked. During the meal there was no conversation and no wine. When the meal was over and all had washed their hands, the party settled down to talk. Now the wine was brought with nuts, olives, fruit, cheesecakes and delicacies like sugar cane soaked in rose

water. The best part of the night was then spent drinking, laughing and talking happily together. Singing girls and musicians provided the main entertainment. You can still hear in Muslim countries the instruments they played: the lute, zither, rebec (a primitive violin), and various flutes, wind instruments and drums. Warmed by the wine, the guests would address love poems to the young slaves who waited on them.

The Muslim attitude to wine was based on what the Koran said. One verse prohibited the drinking of Khamr, an intoxicating Arab drink, and many regarded this as forbidding the drinking of any alcohol. However, Arabia was not a wine-growing country and drunkenness was infrequent there. Consequently, no precise penalty had been laid down in the Koran for wine-drinking. After Muhammad's death his son-in-law, Ali, took a severe view. 'Whoever drinks,' he said, 'gets drunk: whoever gets drunk acts foolishly: whoever acts foolishly lies: whoever lies deserves punishment.' The punishment he ordered was eighty lashes. This might have prevented Muslims from drinking but many judges regarded the sentence as too severe and looked the other way. One judge of Cordoba, on his mule, found himself behind a drunken man reeling along a narrow street. Instead of arresting the drunkard the judge slowed down his mule to a snail's pace, until the man reeled off into a side passage. The prohibition of drinking alcohol in Muslim countries was widely ignored, especially by the wealthy, and the joys of wine-drinking were sung by Islamic poets from Spain to Persia.

Crafts and trading

The Muslims in Spain knew how to enjoy themselves but they were also skilled workers. The great buildings of the palaces and mosques show that. We shall see later (p. 42) that the city was the centre of government and learning for a wealthy and thickly-populated country. It was also a great centre for trade and for the skilful manufacture of beautiful things. Rubies were mined at Malaga, gold and silver and marble at Jaen. Gold and ivory were also brought from West Africa, across the Sahara by camel caravan, then by sea from the ports of North Africa.

Silk was introduced from the East. The cultivation of the silkworm had been for many centuries a closely guarded Chinese secret. Muslims discovered this secret from Chinese prisoners of war when they defeated a Chinese army in Central Asia in 751. This knowledge spread throughout Islamic lands until the silkworm was brought to Spain.

With these precious materials the craftsmen of Cordoba made delicately carved jewellery and caskets, they wove tapestries and carpets in intricate and graceful patterns. They developed the art of tanning and embossing leather for bookbinding, wall hangings and table-covers. They were the first to manufacture crystal. You can see some of the things they made in the pictures below and those on the next page.

opposite: Part of a carved ivory casket, made in 968 for a son of Abd al-Rahman III. In the centre, a musician is playing a lute. One of his companions is drinking wine, the other holds a fan. Behind stands a falconer.

below: A silver casket made in 976, now in Gerona cathedral.

right: The so-called Tapestry of the Witches was made in the twelfth century and its intricate pattern of birds and monsters is typical of Muslim Spanish work.

above left: Decorative wall-tiling from Granada.

above: A bronze fountain in the shape of a stag found at Madinat al-Zahra. The water came out of its mouth.

left: An ivory casket made about 962 for a daughter of Abd al-Rahman III. The Kufic writing going round the box says 'This was made for the noble daughter, the daughter of Abd al-Rahman, Commander of the Faithful, the mercy of God and His approval be upon him'. The front of the casket with its lock is shown here. The size is $1\frac{3}{4} \times 3\frac{3}{4} \times 2\frac{3}{4}$ in (4.5 × 9.5 × 7 cm).

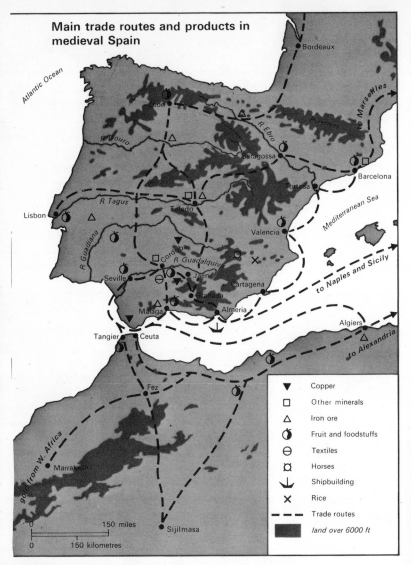

Main trade routes and products in medieval Spain

Atlantic Ocean

Bordeaux

R Douro

R Ebro

to Marseilles

Saragossa

Barcelona

Tortosa

León

Lisbon

R Tagus

Toledo

Mediterranean Sea

Valencia

R Guadiana

Cordoba

R Guadalquivir

to Naples and Sicily

Seville

Jaen

Cartagena

Granada

Almeria

Malaga

Algiers

Tangier   Ceuta

to Alexandria

gold from W Africa

Fez

Marrakesh

Sijilmasa

▼	Copper
☐	Other minerals
△	Iron ore
◐	Fruit and foodstuffs
⊖	Textiles
¤	Horses
↓	Shipbuilding
✕	Rice
- - -	Trade routes
■	land over 6000 ft

0   150 miles

0   150 kilometres

The various crafts and trades which throve in Cordoba were gathered together in particular streets or market squares, just as they are today in places such as Fez and Marrakesh in Morocco. All the shoemakers would be in one street, all the butchers in another and the weavers in a third street (or streets; it is thought that there were 13,000 weavers!). The street names have survived in modern Cordoba, for example Pescaderia (fishmarket) and Cordoneros (lace-makers).

The Muslims made the land produce more too. They dug canals and set up elaborate irrigation systems so that crops would grow in areas where the rainfall was poor. They treated the peasants better, taking less in taxes than the Visigoths, who had treated the peasants as slaves. So there was enough wheat grown to feed the whole of Muslim Spain. They grew grapes for wine, and apricots, peaches, oranges, bananas, figs, rice, sugar cane and cotton. In fact it was the Arabs who first introduced some of these fruits to Europe. Another big crop was olives. Olive trees spread over the slopes of the hills and produced so much olive oil that it could be sent to Africa in exchange for gold. Because the rulers of Muslim Spain controlled this trade, other European countries depended

right: Olive groves in the countryside near Cordoba.

on them for all the gold they received from Africa.

The Arab merchants were in a powerful position. From the great ports of Seville and Malaga their ships took oil, fruit, cotton, sugar and marble for the other Muslim cities such as Baghdad and Damascus. Some Spanish goods even found their way through the ports of Alexandria and Byzantium to places as far away as India and Central Asia. The ships brought back slaves and cloth from Egypt, and singing girls from Eastern Europe, as well as many of the spices and other luxuries of the East.

To protect the trade a strong navy controlled much of the Mediterranean by the tenth century. Abd al-Rahman III had an important naval base at Almeria where he equipped 200 ships of his regular navy. Some words which have come to us from Arabic remind us of this: admiral, corvette, cable, arsenal.

At first the Christians in the north of Spain did not exchange many goods with the Arabs in the south because they were too poor. But by the tenth century they were able to buy many of the beautiful things manufactured in Cordoba. Still, the prosperity of al-Andalus remained the envy of many travellers.

The fame of this city even reached distant Germany where a nun, Hrosvitha (she died in 1002), called it 'the jewel of the world'. 'In the western parts of the globe', she wrote, 'there shone forth a fair ornament . . . a city well cultured . . . rich and known by the famous name of Cordoba, illustrious because of its charms and also renowned for all resources, especially abounding in the seven streams of knowledge, and ever famous for continual victories.'

An artist's impression of the smaller type of ship used by the Muslims in their Mediterranean trade.

4. A society of many races

Arabs and Berbers

Arabs were the leaders of Muslim Spain. They occupied the most fertile lands in the valleys, built the finest houses in the towns, and had the main posts in the government. But from their first entering Spain many of them married local women, so that the population became very mixed. Muslim rulers married Spanish girls who bore them children, until in the end the amirs had little Arab blood in them. Most of them were fair or ginger-haired with blue eyes, not dark-haired like Arabs.

There were never many Arabs in Spain. More numerous were the Berbers, who had formed the bulk of the invading armies. The Berbers were scattered over the less fertile hill country, where they were able to scrape a living by farming in conditions similar to those of their native mountains in North Africa. They were Muslims, but they were loathed and despised by the wealthier Arabs as uncouth barbarians, and were valuable only as warriors. As a result the Berbers felt discontented and were sometimes prepared to take part in plots and revolts against their Arab overlords.

Below the Arabs and Berbers in importance were Spaniards who had been converted to Islam. There was no attempt to force them to become Muslims, but many found Islam attractive if only to avoid the tax which Christians and Jews (but not Muslims) paid. Spanish conversion to Islam was rapid and widespread. Soon Arabic-speaking Spanish Muslims were a majority of the population.

Christians and Jews

Those who remained Christian were well treated, as they were throughout the Islamic Empire. Both Jews and Christians were regarded as 'People of the Book', that is, as people who had their own holy writings, the Old and the New Testaments of the Bible. So long as Christians paid their taxes and did not insult the Prophet Muhammad they could practise their religion freely under their bishops, though they paid special taxes for the 'protection' given to them by their Muslim rulers. In Cordoba the Christians continued to worship in the cathedral of St Vincent, though they were not allowed to disturb the Muslims with hymn-singing or bell-ringing.

Muslims and Christians usually got on very well together, lived much the same sort of life and dressed alike. Muslims took pleasure in attending Christian celebrations and as we have seen were frequent visitors at the monasteries on saint's days. Even warfare did not divide them. Christians in Muslim Spain were loyal to the amir and many fought for their Muslim rulers against the Christian kings of the north. In peacetime Christian kings sent their sons to be taught manners at the court of Cordoba. They married their daughters to Muslim princes and these brides became Muslims too.

Arabic language and literature fascinated Spanish Christians as did Muslim architecture and science. They were so impressed that they imitated the Arabs. Eventually these Christians were given a special name, Mozarabs (from the Arabic *musta'rib* meaning 'Arabiser').

In 854 Alvaro, a Christian of Cordoba, wrote regretfully about the appeal of Arabic to his fellow Christians: 'Many of my co-religionists read the poetry and tales of the Arabs, study the writings of Muhammadan theologians and philosophers, not in order to refute them, but to learn how to express themselves in Arabic with greater correctness and elegance. Where can one find today a layman who reads the Latin commentaries on the Holy Scriptures? Who among them studies the Gospels, the Prophets, the Apostles? All the young Christians noted for their gifts know only the language and literature of the Arabs, read and study with zeal Arabic books, building up great libraries of them at enormous cost and loudly proclaiming everywhere that this literature is worthy of admiration. Among thousands of us there is hardly one who can write a passable Latin letter to a friend, but innumerable are those who can express themselves in Arabic and compose poetry in that language with greater art than the Arabs themselves.'

In the ninth century the archbishop of Seville even thought it was necessary to translate the Bible into Arabic, not so that Muslims should be converted but so that his own community would understand it.

Slaves

At the bottom of the social scale were the slaves. The main source of slaves was war: prisoners were the personal property of the victor. He could ransom, kill or sell them as he wished. Dealers often went on campaigns, so that they could buy prisoners for the slave market. Pirates and traders also imported slaves from Europe, Egypt and the Black Sea ports. A person's religion or race mattered little. Christian slave dealers hired Muslim raiders to capture Portuguese Christians at Coimbra for sale in Spain. The amirs had a liking for fair women from the north of Spain, as we saw on the previous page.

The treatment of slaves depended partly on where they lived. Life was hard for country slaves who worked hard throughout the daylight hours and at night were locked up to prevent them from escaping. The situation of the town slaves, particularly of the eunuchs, was better. Eunuchs were men who had been castrated, so that they could not have families of their own. They could be more loyal, therefore, to their owners – or so it was believed. Eunuchs in the royal palace had particularly great opportunities, as the amirs were not jealous or suspicious of them. Many of them became very powerful as generals, admirals and rulers of provinces. The amir was protected by his bodyguard of slaves who, in addition to serving as soldiers, ran the palace, acted as clerks and did a lot of the routine government work. The country estates from which the amir got his private income were cultivated by slave labour under the supervision of slave overseers.

Female slaves were often very well treated. Bought as young girls, they were carefully looked after and expensively educated by their owners if they showed great beauty or talent. By bearing sons to their masters they often earned their freedom and gained favoured places in the households of the aristocracy. It was a slave girl of Abd al-Rahman III who caused the palace of al-Zahra to be built (see page 18). Dying young, she left a large fortune, to be used to ransom Muslims held in Christian prisons. But there were few Muslim prisoners at this time so her successor as Abd al Rahman's favourite, al-Zahra (meaning 'with the bright face'), proposed that the money should be spent on building a new palace. As this story illustrates, slaves were usually converted to Islam, and when set free most of them made little effort to return to their homeland.

Women

Women in Cordoba might have great influence with their husbands or masters, but they were in an inferior position to men. For most women life centred on the harem, the women's quarter of the house. Here they lived surrounded by other women and children, as no man could enter the harem, except the master of the house. As well as looking after the affairs of the house they would knit, sew and embroider – and no doubt spend a great deal of their time in gossip. A girl brought up in such seclusion would not meet a young man and fall in love. Her father would arrange her marriage for her, before she had even met her future husband.

A Muslim wife had to share the affection and wealth of her husband with the other wives which the law allowed him. The Koran said that 'men are in charge of women' and permitted a man to have four wives if he could afford to provide for them all. And he had to treat them equally and with kindness. If he was wealthy, he could also have as many slave girls as he wished. If a man tired of a wife, he could easily divorce her, without giving a reason, simply by saying three times, 'You are dismissed'. On the other hand, it was almost impossible for a woman to get a divorce, unless her husband agreed. Adultery was severely condemned in the Koran, which laid down the punishment: 'the adulterer and the adulteress, flog each of them with a hundred lashes'.

Yet women, both slave and free, had far greater freedom in Spain than in most Muslim countries. They could walk about unveiled. Slave girls often talked freely with the guests of their masters. Rich women could study in the schools, several of which were open to both sexes.

Basically, though, the position of women and their treatment depended on what the Koran said. This was because his religion was all-important to the Muslim. If he wanted guidance in his daily life he turned to his faith and its holy book, the Koran.

5. The religion of Islam

A muezzin calling Muslims to prayer from the minaret of a mosque.

Faith

As you will have noticed by now the religion of Islam was very important to everyone living under the rule of the Arabs in Spain – either because they practised it themselves or because – like the Jews and the Christians – they admired its effects. What did this religion require people to do? It is easier to answer this question than it is to answer many others about people's lives in the tenth century because the religion of Islam is still practised by millions of people today. It is based on the Five Pillars: faith, prayer, almsgiving, fasting and pilgrimage. The first pillar, faith, is based on the *shahada*, the declaration of belief through which a man becomes a Muslim: 'There is no god but Allah and Muhammad is the Prophet of Allah.' A man had simply to recite the shahada, starting with the words 'I testify', in front of a Muslim and it made him a Muslim too, just as it does today. There were no elaborate ceremonies, such as baptism or communion, before you were accepted as a member of the Muslim community. Once you had become a Muslim you could not renounce your faith. The punishment for doing so was death. There are no priests in Islam, as no man can come between God and the worshipper. Anyone can be the *imam*, or prayer-leader. However, a powerful body of religious scholars grew up called the *ulama* (meaning 'the learned'), who had the same sort of authority in religious matters as the clergy in Western Europe. They had the important task of interpreting the Koran and Muslim traditions and were the spiritual leaders of the community.

Muslims believe that Allah, which is the Arabic word for God, is all-powerful, and sole creator of the world. He is not father of any daughters or sons and so they do not accept that Jesus is the son of God, though they do believe in the prophets

A page from a tenth-century Koran. The kufic script reads: 'So fear God and obey me. No reward do I ask of you for it: my reward is only from the Lord of the Worlds. Do you build a landmark on every high place to amuse yourselves? And do you get for yourselves fine buildings in the hope of living in them (forever)? And when you exert your strong hand, do you do it like men of absolute power? Now fear God and obey me.'

right: A man washes before entering a mosque in Cairo.

and their message. The Koran says, 'We believe in God and that which is revealed unto us, and that which was revealed unto Abraham and Ishmael, and Isaac and Jacob and the tribes, and that which Moses and Jesus received. We make no division between any of them.' Each of these prophets brought the word of God in his own lifetime but men kept straying from it and so a new prophet had to be sent, so men could again find the path to salvation. Muhammad was the greatest and last of the prophets. The word of God, sent through him, would guide men from that time until the Day of Judgement.

The revelations God made to Muhammad were written in the Koran, the Muslims' holy book. The words in the Koran are not, for the Muslim, the words of Muhammad but the words of God and they cannot, therefore, offer wrong advice. Everything stated in the Koran has to be obeyed, as it is a command of God. Muhammad never claimed to have miraculous powers or to be more than human. 'Say "Glory be to my Lord". Am I anything but a mortal, a messenger?' he asked. Yet legends grew up, as they had done round the persons of Buddha and of Christ, which told of his performing miracles. Muhammad did not claim to be a saviour – each

person was responsible for his own conduct to God. He came to guide people to the straight path but others must accept his decisions on matters of faith and conduct, as they came straight from God.

Islam has many ideas in common with Judaism and Christianity. This is not surprising, as in Muhammad's time there were many Jews and some Christians in Arabia, and he would almost certainly have met many Syrian Christians on his caravan journeys to Damascus. Muhammad had never read their Bible but he would have heard about their teachings. In addition to belief in one God and in His revelations, Islam has in common with Christianity belief in angels and in the Last Judgement. After death there will be a Day of Judgement for all men. Then those going to Hell will be separated from the blessed, who will go to Paradise. People used to the barren deserts of Arabia thought of Paradise as a very lush place. 'They shall recline on jewelled couches', says the Koran, 'and immortal youths shall wait on them with bowls and a cup of the purest wine (that will neither make their heads ache nor take away their reason) with fruits of their own choice and flesh of fowls that they desire.'

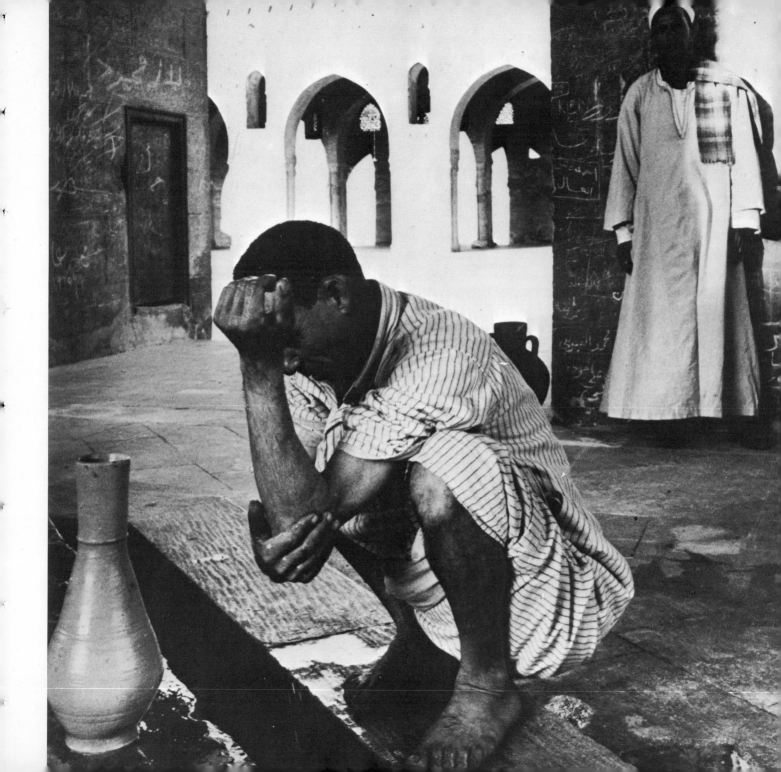

Prayer

The second pillar of Islam is prayer. To a Muslim, prayer is the most important duty of his religion, because through it he gives thanks to God for his existence and all that he possesses. There are two kinds of prayer. Private prayer can take place at any time. Public prayer occurs five times each day. The first prayer is shortly after dawn, when the muezzin's call that 'Prayer is better than sleep' awakens the faithful. The other four prayers take place at noon, late in the afternoon, after sunset and in the early part of the night.

At these times the muezzin climbs the minaret, the tower of the mosque (see page 27), and calls the faithful to prayer saying:

> God is most great
> I testify there is no god but God
> I testify that Muhammad is the Prophet of God
> Come to prayer
> Come to salvation
> God is most great
> There is no god but God.

On hearing the call the Muslim stops what he is doing, and unless he chooses to pray at home, goes to the fountain of the mosque. There he washes his face, his hands and arms up to the elbows, and his feet up to his ankles. If he does not do this he will not gain any benefit from his prayers. This washing is intended to purify a man's body (in the same way that prayers purify his soul), making him physically clean before God.

He then goes to the door of the mosque, where he removes his shoes and covers his head. After entering the mosque, he takes his place in line with the other worshippers facing the direction of Mecca. He begins his prayers standing up, with his hands raised beside his head, palms forward, saying 'Allahu Akbar' — 'God is most great'. He then bows, kneels down, places his hands in front of him on the ground and touches his forehead on the floor, while reciting passages from the Koran. He ends in a sitting position, in which he recites another prayer. Finally, he turns his face to the right and then to the left, each time saying 'Peace be with you and the mercy of God'. According to popular belief, he is addressing angels which rest on each of his shoulders. You can see the different positions in the drawings. The prayers are spoken, not sung; there is no choir, no organ and no singing in a mosque. Women are not allowed to pray with the men but are hidden from their gaze in the mosque, either in galleries or behind partitions.

If if is not possible for a Muslim to attend a mosque at the time for public prayers, he can pray on his own, but once a week — at noon on Friday — all Muslims are expected to pray in a mosque. At this time there is, in addition to the prayers led by the imam, a sermon in which a preacher, often the imam, talks about matters of public interest.

Almsgiving

Giving alms is the third pillar of Islam. A Muslim can give alms voluntarily but in Spain some contributions (collected by the state) were compulsory. They were used to support the poor, widows and orphans, to help slaves buy their freedom and to equip warriors for the holy wars.

Fasting

The fourth pillar of Islam is fasting. Muslims have to fast during the month of Ramadan, the ninth month of the Muslim year, in which God first revealed himself to Muhammad. All except the young, the sick and those on long journeys have to fast throughout the daylight hours of the whole month. Shortly before dawn, Muslims are roused from sleep by a call from the muezzin or by the beating of a drum, so that they can have a quick meal. From the time when the light makes it possible to distinguish 'a white thread from a black one' until sunset, they are to eat and drink nothing. Fasting, like prayer, is supposed to bring a person nearer to God, by reminding him that there are more important things than food and drink. By fasting, a Muslim also learns to understand and sympathise with the sufferings of the poor. As the Muslim calendar is a lunar one, based on the moon, Ramadan does not come at the same time each year. Sometimes it is in summer, sometimes in winter or at other seasons. When it falls in summer the faithful suffer severely, as they cannot take even a sip of water in the heat of the day. For the labourer working in the field, this can be a time of terrible torment.

In Cordoba, after the fasting of the day, the night was spent in a holiday mood. Families came together for an evening meal and after it few people slept. All night the markets and streets were filled with strollers. Children rushed along carrying little lanterns and begging for money. Conjurers and acrobats attracted large audiences, and crowds surrounded poets and story-tellers. The end of Ramadan was the most joyful part of the year, when people celebrated with a feast lasting up to three days. They wore new clothes and exchanged presents just as people in Christian countries do at Christmas.

Muslims all over the world celebrate the end of Ramadan with special prayers.
Indian Muslims in a mosque at Delhi.

31

Pilgrimage

The fifth pillar of Islam is the pilgrimage to Mecca. This takes place in the month of Dhu'l Hidja, two months after Ramadan. At least once in his life, every Muslim is supposed to go on this holy journey to the city where Muhammad had his first revelations. There, thousands of Muslims from different lands come together. All the pilgrims dress alike and perform the same acts of devotion, as a reminder that all men are equal before God. The men wear two simple pieces of plain cotton. One of these they wrap around their loins; the other is thrown over the left shoulder and passed under the right armpit. Women wrap themselves in undyed cloth and cover their faces. In Mecca the pilgrim visits the Kaaba, a large cube-shaped building which, according to one tradition, had been created by God, who built Mecca around it and then encircled the city with holy ground. The Kaaba is covered with a rich black cloth, ornamented with gold bands and embroidered with verses from the Koran. Set in the south-east corner near the door is the Black Stone, which had been worshipped long before Muhammad founded Islam. Muslims

above: A nineteenth-century engraving of Mecca, which shows the courtyard of the Great Mosque full of pilgrims. In the foreground is the Kaaba, covered with a black cloth.

thought it was God's eye on earth. His hand blessed all who touched it. After visits to holy places around Mecca the pilgrimage comes to an end on the tenth day, with the sacrifice to God of an animal, usually a goat or sheep.

Though it is the duty of all Muslims to go on the pilgrimage to Mecca, few from Spain would have had the time or the money for the difficult and dangerous journey. For those who did go it was the crowning experience of their life. They brought glory to their community and great rejoicing followed their safe return.

A small mosque in the desert near Aden.

6. The Mosque

The Prophet's house

One glory of Islamic civilisation is its buildings, particularly its mosques. The word mosque comes from the Arabic *masjid*, which means 'a place to prostrate oneself'. The mosque is a place of worship, as a Christian church is, but when the Arabs first came to build their mosques, they had little experience of building. In northern Arabia the tent was the ordinary dwelling; they worshipped in the open air and the desert sands were their burial place. People who lived in the oases had, as they still have today, crude buildings of sun-dried brick, covered with flat roofs of palm wood and clay, without decoration.

It was from simple buildings like this that the first mosques developed. Muhammad's house at Medina consisted of a courtyard enclosed by walls of sunbaked clay, with huts along one wall. As protection against the sun the flat roof of the building was extended to cover part of the courtyard. The roof of leaves and mud was held up by palm trunks. A palm trunk fixed in the ground served as a pulpit for the Prophet, when he addressed his followers. This palm trunk was later replaced by a small wooden platform with three steps, copied from the pulpit seen in Christian churches in Syria. Muhammad appears to have had little interest in building. He is reported as saying that 'the most unprofitable thing that eats up the wealth of a believer is building'. Yet here, in his house, in its simplest form, is the basic plan followed by all later mosques: a courtyard, some shelter for the worshippers and a pulpit.

33

above left: The Great Mosque at Qairawan, Tunisia, is one of the oldest in North Africa (the present building goes back to AD 836, and some parts are earlier). The features marked are found in mosques all over the world: (A) minaret; (B) open court with wells for washing; (C) covered arcade round the court; (D) sanctuary where people prayed, facing (E) dome over mihrab and looking in the direction of Mecca.

below left: The interior of the Great Mosque at Damascus which was begun in AD 706. Note that there is no furniture and that the floor is richly covered with carpets.

The Great Mosques

As the Arabs advanced into Syria, Egypt and Iraq they came to control people who could build magnificent palaces and churches. When the caliph came to equal in power the emperor of Byzantium and conquered the great Persian Empire, he wanted palaces worthy of his position and mosques which would outshine the most splendid Christian churches and show the superiority of Islam. The caliphs, therefore, took advantage of the peoples they conquered. They brought together artists and craftsmen – sculptors from Syria, wood carvers from Egypt, mosaic workers from Byzantium – from every part of their empire and from lands outside it. These workers built and decorated such magnificent buildings as the Dome of the Rock at Jerusalem and the mosques you can see on the opposite page.

During this time the Arabs added two things which have been a part of every mosque since. In the centre of the wall facing Mecca they built a niche, which they called a *mihrab*. All Muslims turn towards this when they pray and in front of it stands the imam, the leader of the prayers. The mihrab did not contain any statues or image though, like the Christian altar, it was the most sacred part of the church. Because of this, it was usually brilliantly decorated. To draw attention to the mihrab, and to emphasise its importance, a central nave with a high dome was often built, to lead up to it.

The second addition to the mosque was the minaret, from which the muezzin called the faithful to prayer. There were no bells in mosques to do this. The minaret took the form of the watch tower, or its successor, the church tower. In Syria

The *minbar* or pulpit of the Great Mosque at Qairawan dates from AD 862 and is made of wood, beautifully carved.

it was square and this tradition was followed in North Africa and Spain. This was not the only type. Minarets followed the traditional shape of the towers of the country in which they were built. In Persia for instance minarets were round.

35

The mosque at Cordoba

Most Muslim religious buildings in Spain have been destroyed, but one of the earliest and most magnificent, the Great Mosque at Cordoba still stands. When a Christian city surrendered to the Muslims it was their custom to divide with the Christians the chief church of the city. The Muslims then converted their half into a mosque. This happened in Cordoba, where the Muslims took half of the church of St Vincent. When the Muslim congregation grew too large for this part, Abd al-Rahman I sent for the leaders of the Christian Church and proposed to buy from them the part of the building which was theirs. The Christians, after much negotiation, agreed, on condition that they could build a church outside the walls

Plan of the Great Mosque at Cordoba: (a) original building by Abd al-Rahman I; (b) additions by Abd al-Rahman II; (c) by al-Hakam II; (d) by al-Mansur.

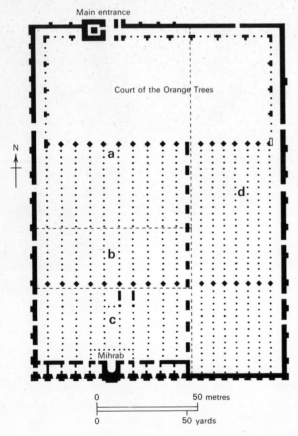

of Cordoba. Abd al-Rahman granted this request, demolished the old church and laid on its site the foundation of the Great Mosque, begun in 785.

Abd al-Rahman aimed to build a mosque to rival in magnificence those of Jerusalem, Damascus and Baghdad. He used all the resources of the district. Strong, long-lasting stone and beautifully veined marble were quarried from the nearby Sierra Morena. Syrian architects made plans for the building and used a number of Roman and Visigothic columns, with carved capitals, to support the roof. As there was such a large space to be roofed, single arches on top of the columns would have resulted in a building that was too low and not strong enough to bear the weight of the roof. This problem was solved, as you can see on the front cover, by using double arches, one on top of another. These gave both extra height and strength to the building. The horseshoe shape of the arches is typical of Muslim architecture in North Africa and Spain though it is thought to have been employed previously by the Visigoths. The idea of using double arches probably came to the architect from seeing Roman aqueducts. Roman influence is evident too in the pattern of the arches: a layer of brick followed by a layer of stone, in red and white stripes.

By the time of al-Hakam II (976–1009), the population of Cordoba was so large that those who met for prayer in the mosque had difficulty in getting in. He, therefore, knocked down the south wall and extended the mosque. In the final enlargement by al-Mansur the builders could not extend the naves already built, as the mosque had reached the banks of the River Guadalquivir. Consequently they pulled down the eastern wall and built eight more naves. This made the Great Mosque the largest in the world. You can walk today through the forest of columns in the mosque, where the twilight beauty gives a feeling of mystery and calm. A thousand years ago the interior glittered with gold, silver, precious stones, mosaics and the light from hundreds of lamps, some made out of the bells taken from Christian churches. The scent of burning aloes and the perfumed oils in the lamps drifted through the arches of the long naves.

To the south of all these columns lies the mihrab, crowned with a splendid dome. This was built by al-Hakam II, who completed the most beautiful parts of the mosque. You can see the elaborate design of the interlocking arches, with carved plaster-work and marble columns, in the photograph opposite.

Part of the decoration round the mihrab. The brightly coloured mosaic work was made by craftsmen from Byzantium. Notice the two bands of Kufic inscription.

left: Arches in front of the mihrab of the Great Mosque at Cordoba. This part of the mosque was built by al-Hakam II between 961 and 965. The decoration is of carved plaster.

Muslim decoration is at its most brilliant in the mihrab but you will notice that there is no painting or sculpture of human beings. No verse in the Koran forbids Muslims to paint living figures, but they feared that this would encourage the worship of idols. There was also a tradition going back to Muhammad's wife A'isha. One day she was making a pillow with a picture on it. 'Don't you know that angels refuse to enter a house in which there is a picture?' Muhammad said. 'On the day of Judgement makers of pictures will be punished, for God will say to them, "Give life to that which you have created".' This did not prevent Muslims painting human figures, on the walls of palaces and in books, but to this day they do not paint them in their places of worship.

A detail of the carved marble near the mihrab in the Cordoba mosque. On the left you can see the decoration above a door in the outside wall.

The Muslims had a passion for surface decoration – coloured tiles, mosaics, carved plaster, wall painting – which makes the inside of their mosques very colourful. A most striking feature of their decoration was the use of texts in Arabic from the Koran. As God had made his revelations to Muhammad in Arabic, the language of the Koran is sacred. Texts from it adorned the mosques, sometimes in the Kufic script (so-called because it came from Kufa in Iraq). You saw an example of this in the photograph on the previous page.

There are no seats in a mosque, as they would interfere with the worshippers prostrating themselves on the ground during their prayers. Because much of the time was spent in kneeling or sitting on the floor, this was richly covered with carpets. The only furniture in the mosque, apart from a cupboard in which copies of the Koran were kept, was a pulpit, usually placed next to the mihrab. From here the Friday sermon was given. The pulpit was usually of wood, with several straight steps, at the top of which was a canopy. The sides of the pulpit were elaborately carved. At Cordoba eight craftsmen spent seven years making the pulpit. It was made of ivory, ebony, sandalwood and citron wood with rails of gold and silver. Unfortunately, when the Christians recaptured Cordoba, this magnificent pulpit was cut up and parts of it were used in the construction of the altar. You can get some idea of the skill and devotion which went into making a pulpit by looking at the photograph on page 35.

Mosques were often fortresses as well as places of worship. The Great Mosque of Cordoba was surrounded by walls six feet thick, designed to stand up to violent battering. Along the walls at regular intervals were forty-eight towers, partly buttresses and partly bastions, most of which have survived. There was no imposing entrance but several doors were placed flat against the wall.

When Cordoba fell to the Christians in 1236, the great mosque was converted into St Peter's cathedral. It then became, and still is, the largest of all Christian churches, except for St Peter's in Rome. Much of the building was changed. The side aisles were removed to make room for Christian chapels and large wall surfaces, beautifully designed and coloured, were pulled down. The worst destruction came when the great choir part of the Christian cathedral was made. In order to build the choir, with its high roof, the Christian architects removed the old ceiling. Three centuries later even so devout a Christian as the Emperor Charles V regretted the change, when he visited Cordoba in 1526 and saw St Peter's choir rising out of the centre of the mosque. 'You have built here', he said, 'what you or anyone might have built anywhere else, but you have destroyed what is unique in the world.' But the great building is still known in Cordoba as *La Mezquita*, the Spanish word for 'mosque'.

An aerial view of the Great Mosque. You can see clearly the Court of Oranges and the parts added by the Christians after they conquered Cordoba: the huge bell tower on the left and the choir rising out of the centre of the mosque.

The Qadi

The Great Mosque was not only a place for worship and for meeting people, it was often the place where the *qadi* (the chief judge) of Cordoba held his law court. He was the most respected of all the caliph's officials, and the only one to enjoy much independence.

The ruler could choose anyone he liked for this position but he took careful note of public opinion. He always chose someone of great honesty, dignity, and of the strictest principles, who could be relied on to speak without fear or favour.

Once he had appointed him, the ruler treated his qadi with respect, even when the qadi expressed an opinion which angered him. A striking story about Abd al-Rahman III, at the height of his power, shows how fearless a qadi could be. The caliph was building, at his palace of al-Zahra, a pavilion roofed with tiles that were plated with silver and gold. The courtiers invited to see this were full of admiration but the qadi remained grimly silent, disapproving of such a show of wealth. When the caliph asked him for his opinion, he replied, 'Never would I have thought that Shaytan [the Devil] had such mastery over you, as to bring you to the level of the unbelievers'. This was a dangerous remark to make to a despot, who was not used to having his actions questioned. There was a moment's acute tension, then Abd al-Rahman gave orders to strip off the offending tiles and replace them with earthenware.

Many qadis, far from seeking the post, did their best to avoid it. They were men of deep religious convictions and felt that, in hearing a case and pronouncing sentence, they were doing what should only be done by God. The responsibility of their position weighed heavily upon them, and more than one longed for the time when he could mount his mule and retire to the peace of his home.

Law and religion were not separate for the Muslim, whose religion *was* his law. Religion was the most important thing in his life and was the guide to all his actions. For all that he should, and should not, do, the Muslim looked to his Holy Book, the Koran. This was the basis of the *shari'a*, the law the qadi administered, a set of rules that governed a man's relations not only with God but with his fellow men too. In addition to the Koran, the *hadith* or Traditions were an important source of law. These were the actions or sayings which were attributed to the Prophet Muhammad by his companions. To Muslims the hadith had a special meaning, as the aim of every believer was to copy the actions of the Prophet in his daily life.

The procedure of a law court was simple. The qadi wore no special dress. He sat or squatted on a bench, perhaps in the shade of the Court of the Orange Trees in the mosque. His secretary and assistants squatted near him. The respect paid by all to the judge was normally sufficient to keep order, but if there was any contempt of court, the offender was whipped. The parties stated their case, followed by supporting evidence. If the judge wished, he consulted his advisers and then delivered judgement. This was taken down and signed by the witnesses, and was carried out on the spot. There was no appeal against his sentence, for although the ruler had to confirm sentences of death or mutilation, and could order the rehearing of a case, he rarely interfered.

Many stories show the fairness of the qadis and the example they set as honest men, who led a simple life. They accepted no pay and many lived in poverty. One story tells what happened when one of the richest merchants in Cordoba died. His slave came to the qadi and swore that, before he died, his master had freed him and told him to marry his daughter. Two Muslims, whom the qadi regarded as men of good faith, swore on oath that the story was true. The qadi therefore ordered that the slave should be free and should marry his master's daughter. Not long afterwards, one of the witnesses urgently asked the qadi to visit him. He found the man dying and in great pain. The dying man dragged himself to the qadi's feet and said, 'Unless you save me, I shall go straight to Hell'.

'This is not so', replied the judge. 'Trust in God and he will save you from the fires of Hell. What weighs on your mind so much?'

'You remember that I bore witness in the case of the merchant's slave? What I said was lies: for the love of God reverse your decision.'

The qadi thought in silence for a time. Then, putting his hands on his knees, he rose and said, 'You must go to Hell. My judgement stands.'

7. Muslim learning

For about 400 years, roughly between AD 800 and 1200, Muslim civilisation was the most brilliant in the world, outside China. You may find this surprising, as the Bedouin who came out of Arabia were nomads with little learning. But they conquered places which had been the home of settled civilisations for thousands of years, particularly Persia and the river valleys of the Nile and the Tigris-Euphrates. They overran parts of the Byzantine Empire where the works of Greek mathematics, such as Euclid's geometry, and philosophy were preserved, many of them already translated into Syriac (or Aramaic, the language Jesus used). As we saw on page 10 the Abbasids built their capital in 762 at Baghdad on the river Tigris. Here the caliphs, especially Ma'mun (AD 813-33), encouraged scholars to translate these books into Arabic. Ma'mun built a House of Wisdom, which was a library, an observatory and a scientific academy. Men of many races and religions came here and helped to make Baghdad a centre of learning. These scholars did not simply repeat what the Greeks had said but added original ideas of their own, so that for over 400 years most of the important work in mathematics, astronomy, medicine, history and geography was produced by Muslims.

They did not borrow only from Greece. Merchants and mathematicians brought from India three things which greatly changed arithmetic: the use of Hindu numbers (nine different signs, as in this picture), the zero and the decimal point. (A small circle or dot represented zero, as it still does in Muslim lands.) These ideas made it possible, for the first time, to deal easily with large numbers. Till then arithmetic, apart from what could be counted on the fingers or on an abacus, was a mystery which only the cleverest understood. With the new numbers, anybody could understand it. A treatise by the Persian al-Khwarizmi, translated into Latin in the twelfth century, introduced algebra into Europe. His algebra was the chief math text book for 400 years.

Persian astronomers also added greatly to a sound knowledge of the skies. Through this knowledge they improved the accuracy of maps and gave the sailor new or better instruments

(a)

(b)

(c)

There are two main Islamic forms of writing: Kufic and Naskhi. Kufic (a) is the earliest form and gets its name from Kufa, a town south of Baghdad, where it was invented. It emphasises vertical lines and was widely used to decorate buildings and pottery. From about AD 1000 Naskhi (b) gradually replaced it, as it has more curves and is easier to write. The easiest script of all to write, and the most graceful, is Nastaliq (c). Here the emphasis is on curves and horizontal lines.

Hindu

Arabic

Spanish

Italian

The new numbers had different shapes in different countries but everywhere there were only nine signs and a zero.

Part of a page from a Latin edition of Abulcasis printed in Basel in 1586. Translated it begins: 'The Method of Curing Several Very Serious Diseases of Women, Especially Those That Need Surgery, Taken from Book 2 of the Method of Healing of Abulcasis, Most Outstanding Doctor Among the Arabs.' The book includes drawings of surgical instruments. Below are two kinds of forceps and a hook.

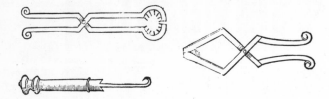

for navigation. One of these was the astrolabe, which helped sailors to find their position when they were out of sight of land.

All this knowledge spread rapidly throughout Muslim lands because of the invention of paper. The Chinese first made paper from hemp, rags and tree-bark about AD 100 but no one knew about it outside China until Muslims, fighting the Chinese in Central Asia, brought some prisoners back to Samarkand in 751. Soon paper was manufactured in Baghdad and, by 950, in Spain. From there it spread to France and the rest of Europe. A reminder that we received our knowledge of papermaking from the Muslims is that our word 'ream' comes from the Arabic *rizmah*, meaning a bundle.

. . . passes to Spain

When the Arabs conquered Spain it was not long before scholars brought Muslim learning to the peninsula. By the tenth century elementary education was general throughout Muslim Spain, except for the poorest. Most boys and girls attended a local primary school, where they learned to read, write, and recite the Koran, before they went on to learn a trade. The rich had private tutors for their children. These youths, who were to become judges, doctors, and civil servants, went to mosque schools after their elementary education. Each quarter of Cordoba had many mosques, which were highly regarded if scholars taught in them. The Great Mosque naturally had the most able professors, both from home and abroad, and by 950 had become a university. It was one of the chief centres of learning

in the world and attracted students, Christian as well as Muslim, not only from Spain but from many parts of Europe, Asia and Africa. Here teaching was given in all kinds of subjects. Most important for the Muslim was, of course, the study of the Koran and the traditions of the Prophet Muhammad. These were followed by Arabic grammar and poetry. The syllabus also included mathematics, astronomy, medicine and the natural sciences. At the end of the course a successful student would receive a certificate similar to a degree from a modern university. To anyone with a certificate from the university of Cordoba, all high posts in Spain were open.

Muslim Spain had a great reputation among its Christian neighbours for medicine. Unlike Christian Europe, where barbers were used as surgeons till the late eighteenth century, in Spain many of the most famous doctors were surgeons. Princes and wealthy men came from all over Western Europe to be treated by surgeons in Cordoba. One of these, Abulcasis, (who died in 1013), carried out many difficult and successful operations in, for example, trepanning, which involved opening the skull to relieve the pressure from tumours. He summed up the surgical knowledge at that time in a book he wrote early

Arab physicians used a wide range of drugs to relieve pain and cure ailments. The drugs were stored in jars like this one from fourteenth-century Spain; height $15\frac{1}{4}$ in (39 cm).

left: This leather book-binding was made in Spain in the fifteenth century. The fame of the Cordoba leather workers was so great that the English called a shoemaker a 'cordwainer'.

in the eleventh century. This was translated into Latin and published in many European countries, even as late as 1778 at Oxford. The book contained illustrations of instruments, which helped to lay the foundations of surgery in Europe. For centuries it was the standard surgical text-book at Italian universities.

Perhaps the most famous thinker and scholar from Muslim Spain was ibn-Rushd, known in Christian Europe as Averroes. Born in Cordoba in 1126, Averroes was a doctor and astronomer but is known best for the commentaries he wrote on nearly all the works of the Greek philosopher Aristotle. Largely through a Latin translation of these works, knowledge of Aristotle passed to medieval Europe.

. . . and then to Europe

The reputation of Muslim universities was so high that early in the twelfth century a Christian monk, Adelard of Bath, disguised himself as a Muslim and went to Cordoba, to study at the university for several years. While he was there he translated into Latin the works of Euclid and smuggled these back to Britain. In this way Greek mathematics began to find its way back into Europe.

After the Christian reconquest of Toledo in 1085, a school for translating Arabic books into Latin was set up there. Scholars came to it from all over Europe. Michael Scot and Robert of Ketton came from Britain and Robert made the first translation in 1145 of al-Khwarizmi's algebra. By 1300 all the important knowledge of Greek science, Arab medicine and Indian mathematics had spread to Europe, but it took a long time before all this new knowledge could be digested. In the thirteenth century a law forbade bankers in Florence to use Hindu numbers. They were not in general use for trade throughout Western Europe for another 200 years.

Christian Europe, then, owed a great deal to its Islamic adversary. Muslim Spain played a vital role in preserving, developing and passing on to medieval Europe the Greek learning that had largely been forgotten there. Without the recovery of this learning and the additions the Muslims themselves made, later European developments in mathematics and science by such people as Galileo and Newton would not have been possible.

8. The end of Muslim Spain

In the tenth century Muslim Cordoba enjoyed its most splendid and prosperous period with two outstanding rulers in Abd al-Rahman III and al-Mansur. It was the most powerful state in Europe, courted by rulers from far and near. At the end of Abd al-Rahman's reign the king of Leon, the queen of Navarre and the counts of Castile and Barcelona, all Christian rulers, recognised him as their overlord and sent him each year a tribute of money. If they failed to pay, the caliph sent his armies to punish them.

Al-Mansur

This strong rule was continued by Ibn abi Amir, who became the real ruler when Hisham II, a boy of twelve, came to the throne in 976. Ibn abi Amir was a great general and won victories against Christians in Northern Spain and against Muslims in North Africa. These victories led him to take the title al-Mansur (the victorious), by which he is usually known. Every year in the spring and autumn he led his troops against the Christians of Leon, Castile, and Catalonia. During these campaigns he sacked Barcelona, razed to the ground the city of Leon with its massive walls and high towers, and even dared to enter the mountain passes of Galicia. In 997 he reached Santiago, the proud city of St James. Christians from all over Europe came here, as they thought it was the burial place of the Apostle James. According to tradition, James had introduced Christianity into Spain. When al-Mansur reached the city the inhabitants had fled. His army took everything that could be carried away and destroyed the rest.

From about 950 to 1000 the Muslims controlled Spain more effectively than at any time before or since. It seemed that the enemies of Islam in Spain had been finally routed.

The situation soon changed.

A pilgrim to Compostella was known by his scallop shell symbol. This twelfth-century statue is at the church of S. Maria de Terra in Zamora.

The collapse of the caliphate

After al-Mansur's death, Muslim Spain was torn apart by civil war. A series of rebellions reached their peak in 1013, when Berbers seized and sacked Cordoba. Al-Zahra and the palace of al-Mansur were destroyed, though the great mosque was spared. One caliph after another was set up, either by the people of Cordoba or by the Berbers. Real power was in the hands of the army. At last, tired of the constant changes, the people of Cordoba decided to get rid of the caliph altogether. In 1031 Hisham III was shut up in a damp and dark vault attached to the Great Mosque. Here, in complete darkness and half frozen, the caliph sat for hours trying to keep his young daughter warm on his chest. Outside, in the city, a public meeting abolished the caliphate. Hisham only begged for a light and a piece of bread for his starving child.

This was the end of the western caliphate and of the great days of Cordoba, but it was not the end of Muslim Spain. When the caliphate ended, Muslims had been in Spain for 320 years. Not until 460 years later would the last Muslim rulers be pushed out of the peninsula.

Out of the ruins of the caliphate arose small Muslim kingdoms which were always fighting one another. Slowly Christians from the north overcame them or demanded a yearly tribute in gold from them. In return they protected the Muslim states from attack. This gold went to the north in large amounts and made Christian Spain one of the wealthiest parts of Europe.

By 1150 there were three large Christian states in Spain, Portugal, Castile and Aragon, but not till 1212 did Christian armies win a decisive battle against the Muslims. In that year a large army, with soldiers from all the kingdoms of Spain and from France as well, defeated the Muslims at Las Navas de

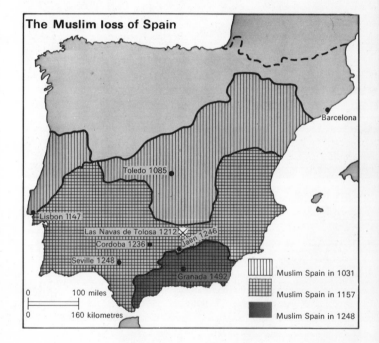

The Muslim loss of Spain

Barcelona

Toledo 1085

Lisbon 1147

Las Navas de Tolosa 1212

Jaen 1246

Cordoba 1236

Seville 1248

Granada 1492

0   100 miles

0   160 kilometres

Muslim Spain in 1031

Muslim Spain in 1157

Muslim Spain in 1248

Tolosa, one of the main passes leading from Castile to the valley of the Guadalquivir. This cleared the way for the Christian conquest of al-Andalus. Cordoba was besieged and captured in 1236. The Great Mosque became a cathedral for Christian worship. Jaen fell in 1246 and the great city of Seville in 1248. In only thirty years all of al-Andalus, except for the kingdom of Granada, had been conquered.

45

The kingdom of Granada

The court at Granada now became the centre of art and learning in Muslim Spain, just as the court at Cordoba had been in Umayyad days. Trade throve, particularly the silk trade with Italy, and made Granada the wealthiest, though not the most powerful, city in Spain.

The Nasrids, who ruled Granada from 1232 to 1492, built the magnificent palace and fortress of al-Hamra (the red), so-called from the colour of the clay used to build its walls. The Alhambra, as the Spanish call it today, is the oldest Islamic palace in the world to survive in a state of good preservation. It was begun in 1248 and took a hundred years to complete.

Although the Christian princes were now stronger than the Muslims, they did not go on to conquer the rest of the south immediately. They spent a lot of time fighting one another.

left: A view of the Alhambra palace from the gardens of the Generalife (there is a picture of these gardens on p. 19). The building at the top left was not part of the Muslim palace but was built by the Christian Emperor Charles V. Below is the Court of Lions in the Alhambra, completed in 1354.

Boabdil, the last Muslim ruler of Granada, walks forward to surrender the keys of the Alhambra. From a carved altarpiece in the Chapel Royal at Granada.

A change came in 1469 when Isabella of Castile married her cousin, Ferdinand of Aragon. Five years later Isabella inherited the throne of Castile and in 1479 Ferdinand became King of Aragon. The two kingdoms, which had been separate for 500 years and had often been at war with each other, were now under the same rulers. Isabella was deeply religious and when the Muslim state of Granada refused to pay tribute any longer she decided to complete the reconquest by driving the Muslims out of Spain altogether.

Her war against Granada lasted from 1481 to 1492. Each spring and autumn her army went on campaign. She had 30,000 troops, some of them highly trained in destroying the crops and water supplies. Because the hills of Granada were dotted with solid stone fortresses Isabella brought in German and Italian artillery which hurled especially large metal and stone missiles. The advance was slow because the army had to build new roads and bridges to take the weight of the heavy artillery. But the issue was hardly in doubt. In 1492 Granada surrendered. This was the end of Muslim Spain.

Glossary

Abd slave

al-Andalus the part of Spain controlled by the Muslims

Allah God

Amir commander, governor. The title taken by the Muslim rulers of Spain from Abd al-Rahman I to Abd al-Rahman III

Caliph successor (to the Prophet Muhammad). The title taken by the rulers of the Islamic Empire in the East and in 929 by Abd al-Rahman III as ruler of Muslim Spain

Hadith tradition: words or deeds attributed to the Prophet Muhammad

Harem the women's quarters of a house

Ibn son

Imam leader of the prayers in a mosque

Islam submission (to the will of God). The religion of the Muslims

Maghrib the West. Part of North Africa controlled by the Muslims

Mihrab niche in the wall of a mosque pointing in the direction of Mecca

Minaret the tower of a mosque

Mozarab Christian in Muslim Spain who spoke Arabic

Muezzin crier: one who calls Muslims to prayer from the minaret of a mosque

Muslim one who has surrendered (to God). A believer in the faith of Islam

Qadi judge

Ramadan ninth month of the Muslim year in which all have to fast

Shahada declaration of belief made by a Muslim

Shari'a the holy law of Islam

Ulama the learned: scholars who interpret the Koran

English words from Arabic

Admiral from amir, commander

Alcohol from al-koh'l, a fine powder used to stain eyelids; came to mean an essence or 'spirit'

Alcove from al-qobbah, a vault, or vaulted recess containing a bed

Algebra from al-jebr, the putting together of broken parts

Apricot is al-birquq in Arabic

Arsenal from dar, a house, and al-cinasah, a factory or workshop

Carafe from gharafa, to draw or lift water

Cipher from cifr, an empty object. Translated into Latin it became zephyrum and later, in Italian, zero. In English both zero and cipher are used

Coffee is qahwah in Arabic

Cotton is qutun in Arabic

Damask means made in or brought from Damascus

Damson a plum of Damascus

Jar from jarrah, an earthen water vessel

Lemon is laimun in Arabic

Magazine from makhazin, storehouses: when used for books it can mean a storehouse of information

Mattress from al-matrah, a place where something is thrown; it came to refer to the thing thrown down, such as a mattress or cushion

Monsoon from mausim, season (hence a seasonal wind)

Muslin from the town of Mosul in Mesopotamia where this woven cotton was made

Orange is naranj in Arabic

Sherbet from sharbah, a drink of fruit juice and sweetened water

Sofa from soffa, a part of the floor raised one or two feet and covered with rich carpets and cushions

Sugar is sukkar in Arabic

Syrup from sharab, wine (in English, a thick, sweet liquid)

Tabby from attabiy, the name of a quarter in Baghdad which made striped silks; thus, in English, tabby refers to a striped cat

Tariff from tarif, what is made known (hence a list of customs duties or hotel charges)

Index

Acknowledgments

Illustrations in this volume are reproduced by kind permission of the following:

p.4 Osterreichische Nationalbibliothek; p.6 Zoltan Berczy (Berber tent); pp.6, 9, 34 (Damascus mosque) J. E. Dayton; pp.7, 28 The Trustees of the British Museum; p.11 Picturepoint Ltd; pp. 12, 13, 18, back cover, Diana Ashcroft; p. 13 map based on E. Levi-Provençal *L'Espagne musulmane au Xe Siecle*, Lerose; p. 15 (mosque court) Courtauld Institute; p. 15 Camera Press; pp. 16, 17, 21, 22 (bronze deer), 37, 38 (marble decoration), 39, 43 Foto Mas; p. 19 Spanish Tourist Office, London; p. 20 Giraudon; pp. 22, 43 (vase) Victoria and Albert Museum; p. 23 J. Allan Cash; p. 29 Roloff Beny Studios; p. 31 Keystone Press Ltd; p. 32 Radio Times Hulton Library; p. 33 F. Rawding; pp. 34 (Qairawan mosque), 35 Roger Wood; pp. 38, 46 Ministerio de Informacion y Turismo, Archivo Fotografico, Madrid; p. 41 Hamlyn Group Picture Library; p. 42 Cambridge University Library; p. 44 Jean Dieuzaide; p. 47 Photo Yan; front cover, Sadea Editores.

front cover: Double arches in the Great Mosque at Cordoba.
back cover: Decorated tile and stucco work beside a door in the outside wall of the mosque.

Drawings by John Holder

The Cambridge History Library

The Cambridge Introduction to History
Written by Trevor Cairns

PEOPLE BECOME CIVILIZED

THE ROMANS AND THEIR EMPIRE

BARBARIANS, CHRISTIANS, AND MUSLIMS

THE MIDDLE AGES

EUROPE AND THE WORLD

THE BIRTH OF MODERN EUROPE

The Cambridge Topic Books
General Editor Trevor Cairns

THE AMERICAN WAR OF INDEPENDENCE
by R. E. Evans

BENIN: AN AFRICAN KINGDOM AND CULTURE
by Kit Elliott

THE BUDDHA
by F. W. Rawding

BUILDING THE MEDIEVAL CATHEDRALS
by Percy Watson

THE EARLIEST FARMERS AND THE FIRST CITIES
by Charles Higham

THE FIRST SHIPS AROUND THE WORLD
by W. D. Brownlee

HERNAN CORTES: CONQUISTADOR IN MEXICO
by John Wilkes

LIFE IN A FIFTEENTH-CENTURY MONASTERY
by Anne Boyd

LIFE IN THE IRON AGE
by Peter J. Reynolds

LIFE IN THE OLD STONE AGE
by Charles Higham

MARTIN LUTHER
by Judith O'Neill

THE MURDER OF ARCHBISHOP THOMAS
by Tom Corfe

MUSLIM SPAIN
by Duncan Townson

THE PYRAMIDS
by John Weeks

THE ROMAN ARMY
by John Wilkes

ST. PATRICK AND IRISH CHRISTIANITY
by Tom Corfe

The Cambridge History Library will be expanded in the future to include additional volumes. Lerner Publications Company is pleased to participate in making this excellent series of books available to a wide audience of readers.

Lerner Publications Company
241 First Avenue North, Minneapolis, Minnesota 55401